The Sword of Eden

The Sword of Eden

Eve and Mary Speak

GRACIA GRINDAL

RESOURCE *Publications* · Eugene, Oregon

THE SWORD OF EDEN
Eve and Mary Speak

Resource Publications
An Imprint of Wipf and Stock Publishers
199 W. 8th Ave., Suite 3
Eugene, OR 97401

www.wipfandstock.com

PAPERBACK ISBN: 978-1-5326-4882-3
HARDCOVER ISBN: 978-1-5326-4883-0
EBOOK ISBN: 978-1-5326-4884-7

Credits: *Theology Today* and *Christian Century*

Cover art: Tom Maakestad

Manufactured in the U.S.A.

For my friends the "old believers" whose conversations and support continued to edify and instruct me over the years

Oliver Olson

Jack and Pamela Schwandt

Walter Sundberg

Contents

Preface

Writing a sonnet sequence is a bold endeavor for a 21st-century poet. The sonnet, in the age of rap, postmodern language poetry, elliptical poetry, and confessional poetry, is not the poetic form of choice for most writers. But Gracia Grindal has deftly joined the ranks of those committed to the tenets of the New Formalism, which Dana Gioia describes as a rebellion against and correction to what was occurring in the poetry of the late 20th century: "the debasement of poetic language; the prolixity of the lyric; the bankruptcy of the confessional mode; the inability to establish a meaningful aesthetic for new poetic narrative; and the denial of musical texture."[1]

Grindal's language is careful, each word chosen for sound and sense. These are poems that are never verbose but exact, the language musical and interesting. For example, the description of Eve's temptation draws us into the scene and presents an idea that is disarming in its freshness: the flattening of the earth after the fall, the dramatic loss of dimension.

> "Reach out, my lovely, toward the web I weave—"
> His tongue glistens with possibilities.
> A globe breaks like a glass of ruby wine
> Filling the fissures of the earth with shade,
> Knowing, I bid my languid lover dine.
> We feed on chaos in the naked glade,
> My appetite gorging on shady night.
> The earth goes flat, the moon a plate of light.

1. Dana Gioa, "Notes on the New Formalism," *The Hudson Review*, Vol 40 (autumn 1987), p. 408.

What is most remarkable is that Grindal makes the oldest stories of our faith—stories we have heard so often that we do not really hear them anymore in their retelling—new, immediate and absolutely captivating.

Contrary to the current fashion, Grindal is not writing poems that are thinly disguised autobiographies. These are not confessional poems, except that poems about women by a woman would naturally show certain predilections that come from shared experiences—even with the mother of the human race and even with the mother of God. Most importantly, these poems provide compelling narratives of two figures—Eve and Mary—who stand alone yet interlink, as certainly they must if Mary is the second Eve. Both, for example, are inextricably tied to the needs and cries of their children. Mary feels the pain of her child's circumcision, and in these poetic lines we also hear the echoes of his future suffering, and hers:

> He wept—
> I saw the dolorous way opening up,
> To suffer his wounds a mother cannot do
> Only caressing him against the hurt
> Sorrow no longer singular, but two. . . .

Likewise, Eve, always a mother, comments in one of these poems about her desire to take on her children's suffering herself.

> Let it be me, I wept, Lord, let their bad dreams
> Shriek in the halls of my head, instead of theirs,
> Let me take up each wound into my bones,
> Puncture my flesh with palliatives for screams
> And let the tubes hanging from their fears
> Enter my veins, stumbling toward you, alone.

What is most refreshing about this collection is its avoidance of the narcissistic tendencies of so much contemporary verse in which meaning is irrelevant or created primarily by the reader's imagination. Grindal *intends* for us to see and to understand. In the final poem of the collection, Grindal writes, "He mothers us, in him we are reborn"—and in that one line is the core of meaning in these poems. These two mothers, one disobedient, the other most obedient, one stepping into darkness outside the gates of Eden, the other walking toward the light her Son emanates, provide the template: we are rooted in this good but fallen earth, as was Eve; and we simultaneously reach toward heaven, as did Mary. Christ, her son, is the mother of our rebirth.

Wallace Stevens has written, "After the final no there comes a yes/ And on that yes the future world depends." Grindal well understands the implications here. The "no" of the expulsion from Eden becomes the "yes" of Mary to the angel Gabriel. We live between "no" and "yes," in the already not yet.

Jill Peláez Baumgaertner
Wheaton College

Introduction

These sonnets on Eve and Mary have been a project of my last few years. Teaching Bible studies that focused on Eve and Mary made me more and more curious about them. While we know much less about Eve than Mary, neither woman has much to say. What they did say, however, has echoed down through Christian history. The church has meditated on them, written on them, painted them, included them in theological commentary and history; both have been characterized in popular and pious history: Eve is to be admired, despite her disobedience. Mary is to be admired for her obedience. Both suffer from cliché existences, Eve the temptress, Mary, impossibly good. Both are pivotal to the Christian faith. Eve is often blamed unmercifully, by especially the early Christian fathers, for bringing sin, and worst of all, sexuality, into the world, though some do admire her for her curiosity, and bravery in reaching out to taste of the forbidden fruit. On the other hand, Mary is seen as holy and beyond reproach. Luther deeply admired and valued Mary as the first Christian in some ways because she bore the Word of God in her body as all faithful Christians do.

The main scene in Eve's life is her decision to heed the tempter's voice and that she blamed him for her fall. We do know that she had three sons, but other than that we know nothing, except as a woman she had a husband, sons, and she watched them grow up. She suffered the sorrow of discovering Cain had killed Abel. Most of the rest of her life we can imagine as being like many women—being in love, mothering her children, raising Seth wondering if he was the promised Messiah, growing weary of her mate, suffering middle age, seeing her son fall in love and marrying, facing old age and death. In a way, her experiences are those of everywoman, something I wanted to explore in these poems.

About Mary we know more. I have used, with some additions, the traditional scenes called the Joys and Sorrows of Mary dear to Marian piety, putting my own Lutheran twist on them. I am most grateful to the book by my friend Lisbeth Smedegaard Andersen *God's Mother and Heaven's Friend: Mary Pictures in History (Guds Moder og Himlens Veninde.)* It has shaped much of my thinking about Mary. My take on Mary is obviously Protestant, but I do appreciate and have learned much from the reverence in which she is held by Roman Catholics and what they have thought about her. One can see evidence of their regard in the thousands of beautiful paintings of Mary which have been painted down through time.

The Marian tradition is filled with conventions and understandings that one can see in any of the paintings. Mary is usually dressed in a blue cape over a red gown. Green foliage for life and white lilies for purity appear regularly in these scenes. She is usually reading a book when Gabriel approaches her. Tradition teaches that she was reading the prophecies of the Messiah. Elizabeth wears gold for her age. For the middle ages, colors, flowers and gems had a mystical language all their own, the meanings of which we have lost, but which are vital to the depictions of Mary. And which we can still read if we know this. Naturally, these many portrayals of Mary, with their brilliant and beautiful colors, were resources for me as were the gems used throughough the Bible as signs of heaven.

Generally, I used the Italian sonnet in the Eve sonnets, and the English for Mary. Both have been popular with English writers since the sixteenth century. Edmund Spenser, William Shakespeare, John Milton, John Keats, and William Wordsworth, and moderns like Edna St. Vincent Millay and Elinor Wiley, have left behind superb sonnets in traditional forms: Spenser, the tightest form with its rhyme scheme of abab bcbc cdcd ee, Shakespeare with his abab cdcd, efef gg now known as either the Shakespearean sonnet or English sonnet; John Milton perfected the Italian sonnet in English with its slightly more demanding rhyme scheme in the octet: abba cddc, and less so in the sestet, efgefg, efggfe, or some pattern like that. The English sonnet form is easier until the concluding couplet at the end which can easily degenerate into doggerel. All of their poems have what the tradition calls the turn, usually between the eighth and ninth lines, whch usually goes back and reflects on the first part, or raises the thinking into a higher plane. This is almost as natural as breathing in and out. The form demands the turn.

The music of the sonnet is to be found in its use of the iambic pentameter line, which is the basic line of English poetry. Fourteen lines, around

140 syllables give or take a few, are what Wordsworth called a "scanty plot of ground." But as he concluded in one of his own sonnets "those who have felt too much liberty/have found brief solace there." Unfortunately, too many contemporary poets have lost the subtleties of iambs, in the search for vivid surprises of thought, rather than in the music of well wrought poesy.

Thinking of the story of redemption from the point of view of either of these pivotal women has enriched my understanding of the Christian faith and helped me to feel more deeply the passion of Christ as his mother looked on. That has been a devotional experience that over the time has been enriching and powerful. It is my hope that these sonnets can cause pondering and wonder in my readers, as they have with me.

I am grateful to Lisbeth Smedegaard Andersen for her exploration of many of these themes in her book on Mary. Additionally, Alice Parker, long interested especially in Eve—her setting of Archibald MacLeish's Eve poems were instructive as were her comments on both collections of my sonnets. Robert Schultz, Professor of English and Poet in Residence at Roanoke College, an old friend and student, helped greatly with the Eve sonnets. Tom Maakestad, the artist whose work graces the cover, continues to surprise with the accomplished beauty of his art. My gratitude to all four is filled with a deep satisfaction that knows no bounds. Most of all I must thank Jill Baumgaertner for reading the work and encouraging me to seek publication. She has been a friend to many a poet over time. For being a friend to me in this process, she has given my work a future, a future I had come not to expect. A poet should not say there are no words to express her gratitude. There are many, the best simply: Thank you.

Gracia Grindal
September 2017

BOOK ONE

The Book of Eve

I

My body turned toward his, my better part
Drawn to the perfect image of my own,
Pulling me toward his dust, bone of my bone,
My bliss, my paradise, my beating heart.
We tripped through Eden, our primeval park,
Mingling our spirits and our flesh as one.
I worshiped his blameless body, him alone,
Mapping our pleasures on a virgin chart.
We played our roles like children out of sight
Feasting on fruit from unforbidden trees,
Tasting the savory dishes of new desire,
Lying beneath a starry quilt of night
Spread out beyond the farthest galaxies,
Our nuptials feted by celestial choirs.

II [1]

"Thou shalt not eat of the golden fruit of the tree
In the midst of the garden," the voice a negative
Of flesh drawn toward the deadly lust to live,
To know, to touch forbidden fruit, to see.
A tongue hisses, mocking the cruelty
Carved in commands only deities can give.
"Reach out, my lovely, toward the web I weave—"
His tongue glistens with possibilities.
A globe breaks like a glass of ruby wine
Filling the fissures of the earth with shade.
Knowing, I bid my languid lover dine.
We feed on chaos in the naked glade,
My appetite gorging on shady night.
The earth goes flat, the moon a plate of light.

---

1. *Christian Century*, February 13, 2018.

III

My eyes opened. I saw him naked, bare,
Apples sweet on our lips, smacking of death,
I tasted it first, rank on my fruity breath.
Twined in our fertile lust, our bodies flared
Frantic to find the world we came to share.
Innocent of Eden, ransacking him by stealth,
We reckoned all our losses as new wealth,
And Paradise a dream we could not bear.
He found us in the garden looking down,
Green with our guilt, baffled by what we'd done.
Nothing to do but suit us up in skins,
Randy and musky in our fragrant sin.
Killing to clothe us, he covered our kindled shame,
Proving us in the angel's cleansing flame.

IV[2]

We blamed each other, fell to bickering.
Who was at fault? Who had lost paradise?
I was the first to fall, to open my eyes.
Back in the leaves I heard the tempter sing
Music of old rebellions, whispering
Soft seductive promises and lies
Buzzing around, Beelzububs of flies.
I had lost Eden for a little thing.
What was the allure murmuring in the trees?
Why had the evil seemed as beautiful
As noxious flowers not yet gone to seed?
Here in the alchemy of sin, our fall
Made visible the midnight where the snake
Teased me with darkness I reached out to take.

2. *Christian Century*, March 28, 2018.

V[3]

The garden flowering behind us, we fussed about
The reasons why, and how we were deceived:
How gullible I was, his gallantries,
Edicts the serpent tempted me to doubt,
The hard scrabble of work. My daily bouts
With tears watering the fragrant leaves
Left me garnering up the yellow sheaves,
Working the human consequences out.
Remembering Eden in each other's arms
We struggled for the paradise we lost.
Too soon the lure of knowledge lost its charm.
Driven together we joined our dust to dust,
Wedding our faults, making our peace again,
Lost in a world spinning beyond our ken.

3. *Christian Century*, forthcoming.

VI

Perchance, I said, and shattered the universe—
Our near relations with the animals,
The blooming vegetables, hard minerals.
Our wills turned against the other's curse,
Mine to a pain that wild desire made worse
His to the daily struggles in the fields,
Eking our bread out of the stony soil.
Sweating against the blame our guilt rehearsed
No balm we harvested could salve our loss,
We hoped for a heel to bruise the serpent's head.
Eating the grain he husbanded for us,
Fighting our flesh, the dream that sin had bred.
We bent toward labor, found it fed our woes
And raised our weapons in the fertile rows.

VII

He could go fishing with the little boys
Teach them how to hunt, how to clean
The fish, and skin the animals for fun.
He'd never been young, except those primal days
Before the gardener took away our toys
And cursed us into working out our pain
Growing among the thistles, bristling thorns—
The kids thought it an Eden, Paradise.
They could be with their father while he worked,
But I was left alone to clean the house.
He was my mother, sister, and my spouse.
I had no company, no friend, no talk,
Only my husband who found it hard to tell
What I meant when I said I'd like a little girl.

VIII

Banished from the garden, and the tree of life,
We walked between the angels' flaming swords
Out into wilderness. The fire roared
As we strode under the banns, husband and wife,
Original in guilt and common grief
We passed our error down, like blooded lords,
Corrupting every man our passion formed.
Each learned the art of killing, the bow, the knife,
Envy raged in the heart of Cain, he killed
Abel his brother, splashing his simple blood
Onto the innocent ground. My fault distilled
The brew they guzzled, darkness become their good.
Chaos broke free, filling the world, my sin
Breeding like vermin, legion, to all our kin.

IX

I was the first woman to fall in love,
To feel my flesh opening with desire
And hear some unnamed music chant like a choir;
Deep in my corpuscles ballads would move
Through me like wind on a silver string that wove
Silken soft webs he could play like a Grecian lyre
Trembling and sympathetic like a wire
Plucked to make melodies only love can prove.
All of my daughters think they are the first
No one can tell them anything, they know
More than their mothers, more than anyone
So they turn slowly like daisies toward the sun
Blossoming shyly not knowing what to do
Fresh and innocent, fearfully unrehearsed.

X

Scripture does not record that I had daughters,
But they are written in my flesh, each one,
Much more difficult than any son.
She floated out of me, up through my waters,
Eager to nuzzle away all that I brought her,
Her little feet padding as she would run
Into my arms. Then, scarlet oblivion
Came slamming the doors on all that I had taught her—
Wondering at the let down, the change in love.
She raged with separation in her blood
Needling my heart with keen jabs of pain.
She broke from me. Like a continent she moved
Into the turbulence of womanhood,
Leaving me rubbing out her crimson stain.

XI

I miss them, their gamey odors, their sweet breaths,
The burbling chatter in the early hours,
Pointing to things skittering on the kitchen floor,
Squeezing a hopping toad nearly to death
To show me the heart beating underneath,
Calling for me to settle up their scores,
The uncomplicated fervor of their wars,
The resoluteness of their true beliefs.
Suddenly they change, turning against my will,
Their fragrances go rank with secrecy.
They battle for their honor and their place
With weapons fired to murder and to kill.
Some wild dispute broke out, all I could see
Was Abel's fall, the fury on Cain's face.

XII

To suffer for a child is worse than death.
I was the first to plead heaven for good
To cool the fevers raging in their blood,
Sweeten the hurt rankling their labored breath,
Master the God in whom I had no faith
But they believed in, their fingers tapping wood,
Gods that the world has always understood,
Whom I bargained with, calling to what's beneath:
Let it be me, I wept, Lord, let their bad dreams
Shriek in the halls of my head, instead of theirs,
Let me take up each wound into my bones,
Puncture my flesh with palliatives for screams
And let the tubes hanging from their fears
Enter my veins, stumbling toward you, alone.

XIII

Breaking the waters of my womb, my son
Lies gasping upon my belly, a small pup.
His hair, wet and wild as a kitchen mop,
Fingers reaching to grasp my own
His eyes the color of primeval stone
Wobbling without my hand to hold him up.
I lift him to the food he has to sup,
His cheeks red, his brow clenched in a frown.
God gave me a son for Abel, and for Cain,
I named him Seth, a gift that God had given
To heal the awful rift, but still my pain
Rips like a fiery sword through the blue of heaven.
What does he know, to think he can replace
My son, his livid scowl, his fall from grace?

XIV

Chattering on about the kids, my plans
To decorate the living room with flowers,
I stopped. He hadn't heard a word for hours,
But sat, looking vacant, like any man
Lost in a world my memory could not scan,
Long before we ambled into Eden's bowers,
Back, way back, before snow or summer showers,
Before the parade of animals began,
Dreaming of water, longing for silence, what?
Regret I had lured him out of Paradise?
Or her, Lillith, my rival—even that?
I could not read the absence in his eyes
So rattled on about nothing at all,
Filling the house with roses, wall upon wall.

XV

Out of the blue, he came and said he'd found
Another love and she was beautiful.
His guilty pleasure grinned like an old fool
Waiting for me to drive his lust aground.
His navy vessels filling with her sound
All decked out, his dingy sails full,
Thrilled he still felt in his flesh primieval rules,
The ropes singing, twisting him around.
My husband, brother, son, and weary mate,
Despite himself he wants me to approve.
Old habits die, their memory a scar.
We peopled all the world with our desire.
Look what he got, the residue of love,
A replica of me without the hate.

XVI

He'd comfort me with apples Sunday night,
Sweet juices tart and tangy on the tongue,
Tasting of those first days when we were young,
Red peelings opening up the flesh of white,
Fragrant with Eden, before I took that bite.
There in the one forbidden tree they hung
Gleaming like ornaments brightly strung
Around the green branches, decked out with light.
New sweet reminders of the world I lost,
There was a hint of Paradise regained,
Promised to us that cursed day he gave
Something more permanent than human love
The services of flesh that still sustain
All the good gifts the tempter tried to cross.

XVII[4]

He kept coming back, hissing in the trees
Whispering sly seductions, making me think
Life would be sweeter if I yielded to his pleas.
Adam grew dull, the children over the brink,
I was his first, he said, "Keep reaching out to take
Fruit flushed with ripeness, you are getting old."
Age drooped before me, remote and bleak,
I longed to taste it, once again be bold.
The little treaties that I made with him
Did nothing, ink spelling out sorrow, pain,
Betrayals to our flesh, hurt to the brim,
Leaving us spent and wasted, praying for rain
To wash away the grievous fault we shared,
The war we waged but never quite declared.

4. *Christian Century*, 2018 forthcoming.

XVIII

Love plunges us toward darkness when we fight.
I did not know sorrow could spring from rage
Sinking to silence, vinting its bitter age.
Pouring its liquor out on the floor of night.
The heart shuts itself down, quenches the light,
Leaving grey shadows dying on the stage
Dark splotches splattered upon a page
Ruined by excess, blemished with unchecked might.
His anger, a blunt weapon to map my soul,
Found new places inside me vacant of pain.
Virgin territories, chaste and whole,
He rode through me like a knight pricking the plain
Hot with his fury, listing toward the dark
Ready to bruise me, thrilled he could leave his mark.

XIX

"It is not good that man should live alone,"
The Lord God said. Without a woman there,
No one will teach him that he has to share.
The plates in the sink will pile up with chicken bones,
His music will drown out the ringing phone
His belly will hang over his belt from too much beer—
He'll do anything he wants, free and clear:
This was the failing the Lord could not condone.
So one day the Lord made Adam fall asleep
As he watched the Technicolor zoo pass by.
The Lord sliced him open, took out a rib,
Shaped it into a woman, who started to sweep
The kitchen, wash the clothes, beautify
The house, making him rise and build a crib.

XX

Waking from Eden, the garden of my bliss,
I panic. Something is breaking, like a glass plate,
Loss hangs in the darkness, formless, without shape.
Where are the boys? I curl into a fist
Hearing the scaly breathing in the mist
That coils around the walls, against the gate.
Still as a serpent, ready to strike, it waits.
I cannot even scream, my lungs resist.
Something is looming before us, I can tell,
Some madman toying with a string.
A woman dressed in dynamite walks by;
Missiles of fire rumble in the sky.
I feel it set its sights, like a cocked spring,
Aiming to blast us through the flap of hell.

XXI

Where he found that girl I'll never know,
But there she stood, blooming at his side.
Fresh as one of Eden's flowers, a bride
In periwinkle blue. Her dress flowed
Like a river of sky beside him, the planets slowed,
Mountains fell, oceans swelled to full tide.
Standing beside the red hibiscus, my pride,
Brilliant, as moonlight dappled them with snow.
Not long before, he fit into my hand
Snuffling like a pup to find my breast.
Holding him close I knew this day would come.
Off to find her in a foreign land,
He'd leave me here, beside the blossoms, pressed
And faded, brimming with tears, quiet—mum.

XXII

The oak, gnarled with many winters, blooms
Its filigree of leaves against the sky
Blue with the fresh spring air of early May.
The bright persuasion of her April groom,
The sun, crossing its Capricorn of gloom,
Pulls life from her dormant beams of grey.
Tender shoots spring toward the pitch of day,
Breaking like morning into a shut up room.
His love, returning with the vernal light,
Wakes my reluctant flesh like buds in spring
Fuzzy with wisps of green, giddy as a girl.
Tipping like earth to face his summer might.
My sympathetic sinews thrum and sing
To the still turning axis of the world.

XXIII

He moved with all his stuff into my head,
White marble busts beside us as we dined,
The black vinyl records of their minds
Turning around the figures while we fed,
Ravishing notes sent from the lively dead.
Food on the tongue along with words and wine
Infinite capacities to bind
One to another, something that we had read
Or maybe heard, thoughts were as physical
As meat, or the table cloth on which we ate.
I added a room made for the word desire
Place enough for his statues and a fire,
Clinking like dinner on a china plate,
Feeding the ghosts grazing in the green hall.

XXIV

The flame banked, the embers glowing red,
We totter toward the end, but still the fire
Heats in my flesh, a memory of desire.
There beside me, him as good as dead,
Our bodies, one sagging flesh that love had bred.
Silly to feel my blood sing like a choir
Chorusing pleasures, hot as electric wire.
I am too old, my laughing daughter Sarah said,
But he is like a comfortable groove,
I know his moods, the force that he is not—
The way he puts me out, the dear old thing,
Setting his cup down, clinking his wedding ring
Against the china, because it is too hot,
Cooling it down, trembling against my love.

XXV

Filled with a rage, searching for what I'd lost
My progeny set sail, trying to find
Pristine Edens as yet unspoiled by lust,
Back where desire and what we had still rhymed
And longing unknown, a place, like Paradise.
They drove their prows into prolific streams
Of new worlds, raised their flags, claimed the prize.
Forgetting ruin festered in their genes,
They killed to store perfection in their holds,
Spreading the dread infection where they went,
Pillaging the innocent for gold,
Tearing a tapestry already rent,
Their native imperfections never healed
The gravity their plunder could not fill.

XXVI

Out of me, a vine, umbilical,
Rich with our fault, the afterbirth of pain,
Trail out the lot of them, original,
With imperfections all their own.
A filament of terror, bent on ruin,
Ready to build battlements to save
All of the dread conviction in their bone.
Nothing before them but a stony grave.
Armies rumble across my unsigned dust
Blasting away for dominance, young blood
Seeping like pools into the ancient must.
Those who are left, weep in the twisted wood
Waiting since Eden for another chance,
To clear the line of sin's bleak evidence.

XXVII

Where, underneath the wrinkles, the sagging skin,
The rotund belly, has he disappeared?
The blonde Adonis of our nimble years
Has built a bulwark over the quick within
As if to dull the sharp knife of old sin
And drown the hidden spring of quiet tears
In a flood sweeping away sensation's fears,
A brew to numb his conscience and its din.
Like Michaelangelo, can we go back
And find the form sleeping inside the stone
Waiting to be released by a skillful hand,
To leap out firm and fresh, with nothing slack,
Freed by the chisel from all that we have done,
The appetites that feed and shape a man?

XXVIII

Nothing sings sweeter than lost innocence.
Things I thought hard or solid as ancient oak
Shifted beneath me, fading like distant smoke.
Love, once a bulwark against concupiscence,
Went flat as beer and did not come again.
The children wandered off to other folk,
The ark we built to house them, an antique joke,
The legacy of Eden gone in a glance.
I broke the rule that kept the harmony
Singing its hymns of glory to the spheres.
None of my children know the pain I flee.
I lost the music they can never hear:
A sweet strain playing melodies of loss
Echoes from stations we can never cross.

XXIX

Days turn into years, feelings into flesh.
Our ceremonies mark the passing time:
We toast the calendar with vintage wine,
Marking the memories that sparkle and flash
In the mind's camera, moments as bright and fresh
As cut flowers, a burst of light, a sign
That life pushes toward fullness, then declines,
Brightly, like orange berries on the ash.
Against this awful progress we have love,
A promise that endures across the years,
That builds toward ripeness even as we fail.
The losses take their places as we move
Toward pleasures that we set against the fears
Greeting us as the dark shutters and falls.

XXX[5]

The destination shines like a sun before us,
Outside the scenery flashes, gardens of green,
High topped snowy mountains, bright and glorious
Oceans crashing against a clam shell beach.
The beauties of the earth are Paradise
Until the silver autumn dies away,
Leaving black branches bare against the skies,
The waste of nature's prodigality
Scutttering at our feet. Our mortal flesh
Cannot outlast the seasons of its frame;
We come like summer to the morning, fresh
As dew on new leaves pearling at heaven's rim.
Only the gleaming ports ahead can move
Our bones corruptible toward what we love.

5. Grindal, Gracia. "The Wisdom of the Wise," *Theology Today* 62, 1, p. 89. Copyright © 2006 *Theology Today*. Reprinted by permission of SAGE Publications. http://journals.sagepub.com/doi/10.1177/004057360506200114.

XXXI

We had not learned the intricates of death—
Pioneers in the virgin land of age
The misty dark, where no mortal had gauged
The distances; children and friends like wraiths
Watching our flesh give up its final breath
Wondering at the progress of each stage.
No lessons to read graven on a page
Instructing us in the practices of faith.
We felt something brushing its feathery wings
Over our bodies, a black shadow, pain
Grinding its pitches in our stiff-boned knees,
Swollen knuckles bulging around gold rings,
Uncertain sounds—applause or summer rain—
And shades looming over us big as trees.

XXXII[6]

We bring nothing to our rendezvous with death—
A wealth of medicines cannot redeem
Our flesh turning to marble in its seams
Breaking down into a rank, foul breath.
None of the arsenals of force or blind faith
Can beat the monster back or kill his schemes;
He stalks about the fortress of our dreams,
The heaven we have built upon the earth,
Tearing it down like tiny paper toys.
The wisdom of the wise is soon undone.
Our purse is empty. All we can do is hold
Our hand out to receive much more than gold:
A testament bright as the morning sun
The coin of the realm where death has been destroyed.

6. Grindal, Gracia. "The Wisdom of the Wise," *Theology Today* 62, 1, p. 89. Copyright © 2006 *Theology Today*. Reprinted by permission of SAGE Publications. http://journals. sagepub.com/doi/10.1177/004057360506200114.

XXXIII

Eden behind me in its musky myth,
They buried me, leathery skin and bone
Near the fertile fields of Babylon.
Mother of all the living, sin and death,
Bred from his bone, Adam, the scion of earth,
Back to the dust to which we all return.
I watch my children join me, one by one,
Crossing the threshold with one last gasping breath.
There is no stone marking my unknown grave,
Only the monuments they raise to mark
Conquests no one remembers in the sand—
All of it caused when I reached out my hand
To taste of knowledge, innocent of dark,
Sure that my disobedience was brave.

BOOK TWO

Mary Ponders

I

Annunciation

Now soft! The blue settles over my head
While the leaves of my book flutter like birds above me.
The air splits with a light as bright as God
And standing before me a brilliance that stirs and moves me.
I feel a presence, a voice older than Eden
Rising from the pages in my hand
That bows and speaks an old familiar greeting
Then makes the strange proposal with no demand.
Its brightness dazzles with words too strange to bear,
He waits my answer. The universe is still.
Breathless I listen as the rolling spheres
Pause, expectant and silent before my will.
A fragrant lily trembles at my side
As words pearl from the past into fields of light.

II

Eternities cascade before my eyes,
The scent of evergreen beside a stream,
Forbidden trees, the fruits of paradise.
A sad and silent couple like a dream
Walks from the verdant garden, hand in hand,
The promise of a heel and trampled head,
Hope while they toil and labor without end.
Crying in the desert the prophets see a maid,
An innocent whose yes will change the world
And mend the image sin has rent apart.
With my assent, I feel the cosmos whirl—
The sword of Eden piercing my trusting heart
That flesh again, a woman by a tree,
Can bring to naught the girlish yes of Eve.

III

Fresh fruit flickering in the blooming leaves,
She looked with hunger at it, heard the voice
Tempting her, I will be human, I will be Eve,
And reached for life, not death, she made her choice.
Her yes was no to him who walked the garden.
In seizing life our mother seized on death.
The Lord now asks for help to work a pardon,
Restoring paradise to life on earth.
Here in the blue, my heart beats warm and red,
The passion Eve desired, I have not known.
I've heard it's our refusals we regret,
What might have been failing a stubborn no.
He stands and waits my answer. Can I trust
A promise mingled with old Adam's dust?

IV

A door opened which never can be shut.
History rolled itself out of me
Unscrolling back to Eden, Eve's reaching out
And forward to a place I cannot see,
Where light gathers itself in flights of gold
And holds all things together, bound by love,
Its ending and beginning. The angel told
The miracle, now speech itself has proved
Its force to shape the future of the world,
The cosmos, all creation, out of time.
It moved through me in waves, a word uncurled.
A day that will be noted, bells will chime:
When vast infinity found place on earth
Joined with my body, waiting a timely birth.

V

Visitation

Startled by what the angel Gabriel said,
Assenting to the miracle, I ran
To visit her, the old Elizabeth
Up in the country hills of Judah's land
To prove the angel's message sound and true.
Breathless, I saw her waiting at the door
Holding her hand on her belly, then I knew
That I should be the mother of my Lord.
Her flowing robes of gold enveloped me.
Quickened, the baby kicking in her womb,
Pointed to mine. Her wizened eyes could see
The promise kept—there in the pitch of youth,
A turbulence, my face scarlet, flushed,
The clangor of my heart not to be hushed.

VI

My time had come, lifting me from the curse
And Joseph knew, putting me away
In Judah where Elizabeth could nurse
My panic, helping me to face the day.
The child in her, impossible but real,
Gave her the faith to recognize her Lord
Gotten in me, knowing how I would feel
Betrothed to spirit, changed by an angel's word
Yes taking form within my virgin womb.
A scandal, Joseph losing faith in me.
The consequence filling every room
A son playing with wood beneath a tree
Facing me with the fate all women know
That moment saying yes instead of no.

VII

Suddenly my destiny was not my own,
Knit to another by natural bonds of flesh
Whose ends loomed in the distance, bright, unknown.
Fear and hope dazzled me, far ahead.
Ancient prophecies in me fulfilled:
A force from Eden whose end I could not see
As the donkey carried me up over the hills
To Bethlehem, Egypt, Gethsemane,
Swords flashing, angels, blood, and me a maid
Dreading the awful dawning of my son.
Women since Eve had hoped to bear this seed
Generations longing, I was the one!
The fullness of time took shape within my womb,
Hope dancing before me, an empty room.

VIII

Joseph, my promised, decent, kind and just,
Rocked by the news of the unexpected child,
Resolved to send me home, how could he trust
The story I told, delusional, and wild.
Tossing and restless, he heard an angel speak,
Over his sleep. Brooding, sick with new woes
Waking him into a world he could not dream.
Trusting the words that men can hardly know,
Filled with the oracles he knew by heart,
He rose to burdens, travels he had to take.
Weary journeys, blood and sorrow, hurt,
A word looming before him, for my sake
He traveled down that road, looking to spy
The revelation, the end of prophecy.

IX

Nativity

South through the dusty heat, our time had come.
Moved by the wheel of empire, always turning,
The ripeness of my body, we left home.
The donkey plodded on, my stomach churning.
Up hill and down, I knew, like every girl,
My body, hosting infinity itself,
The forces of nature, all that rules the world.
Pushed by the Roman decree beyond our help.
A little family, simple as garden fruits
Holding the secret of the universe
In their seed, words like vegetable roots
Grew in us, Eve reaching out, the garden curse,
The promise to Abraham, Isaiah's woe,
Caesar, the angel, nothing to do but go.

X

The skies, fading toward night, a royal blue,
Stars singing like angels far above,
We entered Bethlehem, no room in view.
Each place filled up, not ready, my hour had come.
Panicked with pain, my mother far away,
Nature took over, the baby would be born.
An innkeeper saw my state and pitied me,
Back in his stable, beside the beasts, the corn—
Joseph made place for me, blankets for a bed.
One with the dust strewn over fragrant hay
Its sweet aroma, where the animals fed.
The brute force of nature had its way.
Water breaking, waves in my body, my blood,
A child, bone of my bone, broke like a flood.

XI

We swaddled him, laid him in the manger
Heaped with the hay the animals would eat,
Their lowing stopped. They knew this human stranger
Lying where they snuffled out their feed,
His cries, a voice that all the world would know.
An ancient urge pulsed in my youthful flesh.
He called me toward him, soon my milk would flow.
Something had ended, I moved toward the creche.
Lifting him up, earth and all heaven moved.
The child I held—the costly, precious pearl—
Displaced, I'd given all for him, a love
Large as the heavens, changing me from a girl,
Woman now ready and grown to take my place
In the homely work of nursing my son, his grace.

XII

The Shepherds

The stars, they said, the stars burst into song
Great lights spilling over nutritious fields
Turning our hopes to speech, for what we longed.
"Fear not!" but fear buckled their knees, they knelt
Before this song, after centuries our night
Of sorrow ended, and endless day had come.
Heaven floated down, filling the skies
With shelves of light. Here God had made his home,
Now made flesh suckling at my breast
As they tumbled toward me to see my newborn son,
They bowed toward beauty in this house of bread
The food we lived on. Here with this little one—
The shepherds, animals munching, sweet smells of milk
God growing under our skin, softer than silk.

XIII[7]

The let down, my milk coming in, the shepherds gone,
Music like silver impressed on the skies above
Here in this infant, the tempter's curse undone,
Divinity now lying in the rough—
A stable, the friendly beasts, our flesh like theirs.
Young as a bud, I pondered what this meant:
The baby in my arms, God unawares
Rooting around to find my virgin breast
A wonder every newborn mother knows
Feeling his perfect form growing from me
Made in my image, fresh as a summer rose
It happened in me, without me, stunned, I could see
How nature works through us, our carnal ways,
A permanence that stamps and spends our days.

7. *Christian Century*, December 5, 2017.

XIV

Out of my waters, he lifted him and named him,
Jesus, so spoken, it was, there in his arms
Joseph took him as his own and claimed him,
Taking his place as father, there in the barn
The house of generation, a promise kept.
Safe in his care, I marveled, our marriage bed
A stable. Chastely we lay and hardly slept
The baby nuzzling me, our closeness bred
Flesh into dreams as we held each other near
He reigned between us; learning to live for him,
We fed him, washed his diapers, dried his tears,
Versing ourselves with babies in Bethelehem,
Changed by the angels who drew our bodies forth
Into the services of heaven and earth.

XV

The Magi

Odors of Arabia drifted through the stall
Three sages or magi, kings, came striding in.
Divining the star, they could not dim its call:
Over the stinging sandy wastes these kings
Drove their huge camels westward into the sun.
Now with their gifts they knelt before my child.
One gave him gold, ready to forge a crown,
Then frankincense to signal a sacrifice.
Born to be offered on a day called good
Innocent of foresight, despite my callow youth,
I shuddered to sense the fate of my very blood
From those reading the stars for living truth
Like rich perfumes that overpower the worst,
Transport you back to moments, the very first.

XVI[8]

The third sage brought us myrrh for his mortal flesh
Wrapped up in strips of cloth to ward off the stink
Cadavers make in the grave after death,
Harbingers for my son, unlikely king.
Bitter its fragrance, filling that house of birth.
The odor of death mixing in with old perfume,
Graves dug into the side of humble earth.
Later inside an unused marble room
Swaddled in linen, ready for us to lave
His familiar limbs with costly oils
The scents, omens the third wiseman gave
Now rising up from Eden's garden soil,
Covered up my son in the linen shroud,
All faith and hope drifting around my doubt.

8. *The Christian Century*, December 20, 2017.

XVII

The Circumcision

The first cut, blood, dark waters running from his veins
Flowing from Eve through the line, bridegroom of blood,
From Abraham to Moses, a tangled skein
Hurting he wept for me to give him food.
Tears for his pain, salt on my cheeks and lips
I held him, knowing the ceremony cut
The covenant into his flesh. He wept—
I saw the dolorous way opening up.
To suffer his wounds a mother cannot do
Only caressing him against the hurt
Sorrow no longer singular, but two
Separating slowly at the heart,
Each day growing away toward his death
I held him close, on the lintels of my breath.

XVIII

The Presentation

He met us with a song his body knew
Mouthing the prophets' cries in his prayers.
His hope visible, his death coming into view.
He took the baby, blessing him, long prepared.
Chanting a verse I never would forget—
Swords piecing my heart, the old man sang,
Seeing the thorns, the lance, the blood he shed
On the cross. Far away bright weapons clanged
We offered our sacrifice, two turtledoves
Cleansing me, bringing me back to the rites.
The temple's golden light glimmered over us
Singing for love, holding the world's true light
Wondering at the ruddy child he held
Doing our duties, the prophecies fulfilled.

XIX

Flight to Egypt

Flee! King Herod heard the wisemen tell
Of a king's nativity in Bethlehem.
Murderous with power, the potentate cried. "Kill!"
Newborn baby boys threatened him
Sweet in their mother's arms, ripped from their hands.
Joseph, dreaming of danger, took us south
To Egypt, like Moses fleeing Pharaoh's commands.
Riding the donkey jogging me back and forth,
Panicked by sights of soldier's swords and shields
We fled, nature's cycles rolling by
Riding along the greening barley fields,
Emerald grain under a topaz sky,
Nodding their blades of foliage in the breeze
Innocent of Herod, his steel decrees.

XX

The Holy Childhood

Twittering like a bird at the pink of dawn
He learned his mother tongue, every name
All that he touched, old Adam's perfect son.
Playing in the dust from which we all are made
Feeling the timbers, brandishing them for swords
Tripping toward danger with quick little steps.
I kept him safe, holding him back with words
Yes to the angel, now negatives passed my lips,
Love made me cross, agony he could hear.
All mothers know the child is not their own.
Writ on our flesh, the rule of all the spheres
They come with pleas each school girl needs to know:
Our deepest urges, irrisistable and wild,
Give us the tending of a needy child.

XXI

Jesus, Twelve in the Temple

Distracted, we lost him there in the Passover crowds.
Festivity filled us with forgetfulness
Hand to hand, telling stories, familiar, loud,
We left Jerusalem for Nazareth.
Suddenly the boy vanished, gone from our sight.
Running against the thronging crowds for him
Our son, disappeared and lost, we missed his light.
Turnng over the stones in Jerusalem—
The temple! Frantic and breathless we found him there
Teaching his elders what they understood,
Right at the heart of what any scribe could bear.
Worried and angry, I saw my flesh and blood
Taking over his heavenly father's trade
Wondering at the radiance his presence gave.

XXII

Wedding at Cana

Ceremonies swirled around us, the wine, the dance
Family, friends, the whole village came.
Spirits rose, the shattering of the glass
Marking a sorrow ahead we could not name.
Shouting, laughter, suddenly the wine all gone
Aunt of the bride, the banquet duties mine.
Almost strange he entered, grown man, my son.
I beckoned. "Woman, it is not my time."
Familiar the look that fathomed something more.
"Do as he says." Water brimming over stone,
"Give them to drink," he said. We watched them pour
Wine, rich in purples, vintages unknown.
The best for last, we circled the bride and groom
Like heaven, wheeling around the golden room.

XXIII[9]

Jesus Returns to Nazareth

He fought with dragons in the wilderness,
The old Nick, he who had his way with Eve.
Jesus, my grown son, now in Nazareth,
In the synagogue, they never believed
I mothered him. Crazy, the family thought.
The crowds parted announcing his family neared.
Murmuring at the mysteries he taught.
He peered through the crowd, wanting me to hear:
"Who are they? Those who do God's will are mine,
My mother, my sisters, my brothers, all of you,"
I watched him change the seed to bread and wine,
His heritage made words riding the blue.
My son now giving birth without the seed
That I had gotten him for, out of godly need.

9. *Christian Century*, March 28, 2018.

XXIV[10]

Palm Sunday

Watching people flock to hear him preach
Holding their limbs up to be touched and healed,
I pondered again the love I heard him teach,
Knowing his enemies wanted to kill
My son reverenced the heart, the very truths
They held against him now. Puzzled, amazed
At all he knew, his purity of youth.
I saw him, following him that deadly day
He rode like David through the crowd, a king.
Hosanna, they shouted, throwing their garments down.
My flesh made strange, I felt my body sing,
Palms now a green road as he swept into town
A Caesar, soon to hear his subjects cry—
My Lord, my own sweet child—be crucified.

10. *Christian Century*, March 28, 2018.

XXV

The Trial and Mocking of Jesus

Waiting in the shadows with Peter standing near
I saw them mocking him with a crown of thorns
Pressing it on his scalp, blood dripping like tears
Cruel crowds taunting him that Friday morn,
Weak Pilate pointing to him, Behold, the man!
Taking the pain for me, I could not help.
All the agony of mothers who stand
Seeing their children suffer as no one else
Cutting their hearts as they weep and pray
"Make his torments cease!" The prophets foretold
That whips would stripe his body, his wounds would splay
His back festering, the curse as old
As Eden, our parents being forced to flee
The garden my son was battling to redeem.

XXVI[11]

Via Dolorosa/The Veronica

Mother of sorrows, I followed in his way
Seeing him stumble beneath his heavy cross
Weeping at the agony of this awful day.
More than a sword pierced my heart, my loss
Staggering beneath the shame of all the world.
Delusional, face pouring with blood and sweat
He bent to have his face wiped by a girl
Leaving its imprint so we would not forget.
Running my fingers over the impressed face
I draw the brow, like mine, now bruised and dark,
His noble mouth, my father's. I could trace
All of our people, all of the family marks
But something else, I heard it when he cried,
The voice, his father's. The God they would have die.

11. *Christian Century*, March 28, 2018.

XXVII

The Crucifixion/Last Word to Mary

They hammered huge spikes through his hands and feet
Nails ripping at flesh, the hurt, the pain.
Hanging above me, hardly able to speak
He looked at me through a hail of bloody rain,
Beside me his beloved friend. He gasped
His word to me, "Woman, behold your Son!"
Struggling for breath, his strength ebbing and past
"Take her as your mother!" he mumbled to John.
Exhaling, his duty ended, something new.
Etched by speech making us all his kin.
Out of his body, physical and true,
His words created worlds of love again
With his last sighs he breathed and made us one
Grafting us into his life, his flesh, his bones.

XXVIII

Death, Deposition of our Lord

His father could not abide the stench of sin
Abandoned him, leaving me alone,
Hearing him breathless, gasping short and thin.
He gave up the ghost. Dead. Breath I'd known
Finished. He slid awkwardly into my arms,
I cradled him like a baby, stiff in death,
Soiled by human pain, beyond all fear of harm.
Nothing, nothing, Did I hear a little breath?
His vision dead and vacant as he cooled.
My body's heat useless to raise him up.
He lay in my lap, blood at our feet in pools.
I bore him now in death, barren of hope
Winding his body with white linen clothes
Swaddling his decay. The tomb was closed.

XXIX

The Women at the Tomb

By early light—we had not slept a wink—
We left with spices we'd prepared to lave
His body, annointing it to cover the stink.
His corpse stiff, marble where he lay,
The final rites, investitures of loss.
We rounded the corner—the great stone had been moved.
We found only the neatly folded cloth—
Had they stolen the body of the one we loved?
Sound split the rocks, "He is not here, but risen!"
Alive! Stones blossomed like a lily field
All my expectations broken, riven
The hurt like blades cut me, could I be healed?
Not dead? All of nature overturned
Tombs flowering, within our hearts a fire burned!

XXX

The Resurrection: Christ Appears to the Disciples

The wounds made whole and healed, marking him still.
His body I knew, now radiant as a gem
Come from a new world, difficult to tell
The prophets dreamed it bright as a diadem.
Bowing to his flesh gleaming with light.
As mother I worshiped him, my son, my Lord,
Angelic messages, amythyst and bright,
Annunciations, grief, death, a sword,
Shining a golden jasper in the room.
Spirit tangible in risen flesh
From Eden a promise resident in my womb
Glowing with Paradise, the first day, fresh,
In his bright eyes heaven danced and spun with sound,
I tippled with Hannah, thankful for every round.

XXXI

The Ascension

Forty days, he left us for the skies,
From a green mountain outside Jerusalem.
Blessing us, be fruitful, multiply
Making disciples to serve and follow him.
Adam's progeny knit to flesh, now made
Children born of water and the word.
Old nature out of Eden still held sway
But seed passing into promises we observed
His coming kept the prophecy to Eve
Reclaiming the paradise that she had lost,
A new creation. I had to watch him leave,
To vanish; my crimson heart peered across
The edges. "Always, I will be with you."
My son faded, up, and out of view.

XXXII

Pentecost

He breathed his spirit in storms over us
Still in the Upper Room, bereft, in prayer
For comfort, feeling alone, since the cross.
They held me close, salving my grief with care.
Winds rushing in with tongues of fire, we spoke,
His absence palpable still not the same
But present, filling the room, our bodies shook.
He hovered over us, we said his name
The promises of Eden coming true.
To give him up for all the world, I did
As every mother does, but hates to do.
Only by Spirit could he dwell with us and live
I felt him near, dwelling in my heart
Raptures of heaven in every blissful part.

XXXIII

Mary Old

To ponder, turning over and over thoughts
Like gems, watching facets sparkle as they turn
Wondering at the news the angel brought
My yes at the heart—the diamond flashes and burns.
For every girl hearing she will give birth
A door opens, nature takes her up
Into its swirl, human, shaped out of earth,
And Spirit bright as sapphire, breath and hope.
I harbored in my womb the Son of God.
Flesh to the marrow, seed from old Adam's line
An ending to the tree, the tracing of blood.
His body given now in bread and wine.
Patient I wait, pondering the shafts of light
Radiant in the dust, to see him right.

XXXIV

Mary's Death

To be human, bodies filled with the breath of God,
Dwelling nearer to him than to ourselves,
God coupled with flesh. Heir to my blood,
Like me, my son, image of God himself,
But truly human, death written in his bones
The sentence after the tempter's conquest of Eve,
Giving us new hearts, flesh instead of stone.
Mother of God, haggard and old, I leave,
Trusting my son to raise me into light.
Earth quaked and gave up its dead that early morn.
His death agonies, birth pangs for us that night.
He mothers us, in him we are reborn.
My eyes close. The light around a corner bends
Shining, opening before me, it never ends,